CRASH COURSE IN SCALES

BY BRENT EDSTROM

C major scale

Mixolydian mode

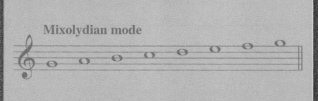

A harmonic minor scale

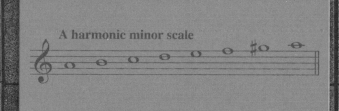

C blues scale

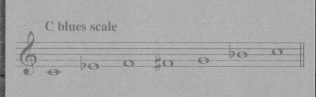

C natural minor scale

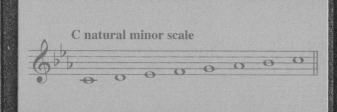

whole tone scale

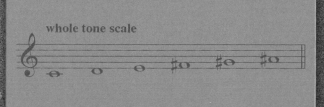

C pentatonic scale

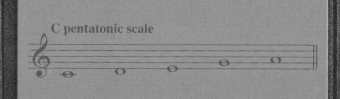

Hungarian minor scale

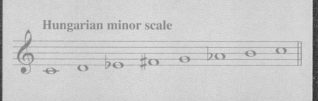

ISBN 978-1-4950-0972-3

HAL•LEONARD®

Visit Hal Leonard Online at
www.halleonard.com

Contact us:
Hal Leonard
7777 West Bluemound Road
Milwaukee, WI 53213
Email: info@halleonard.com

In Europe, contact:
Hal Leonard Europe Limited
42 Wigmore Street
Marylebone, London, W1U 2RN
Email: info@halleonardeurope.com

In Australia, contact:
Hal Leonard Australia Pty. Ltd.
4 Lentara Court
Cheltenham, Victoria, 3192 Australia
Email: info@halleonard.com.au

CONTENTS

UNIT 1: GETTING STARTED

What Is a Scale?

A musical scale is formed when a collection of notes is placed in ascending or descending order of pitch, as shown below. The word scale comes from *scala*, the Italian word for ladder; it is easy to see how the resulting scale resembles a ladder:

One of the many ways that scales are useful is as an analytical tool to provide insights into a composition. The following excerpt shows how a scale could be formed from the notes of a piece of music. In this case, the resulting scale provides important information about the melodic and harmonic resources that J.S. Bach used when he wrote this piece:

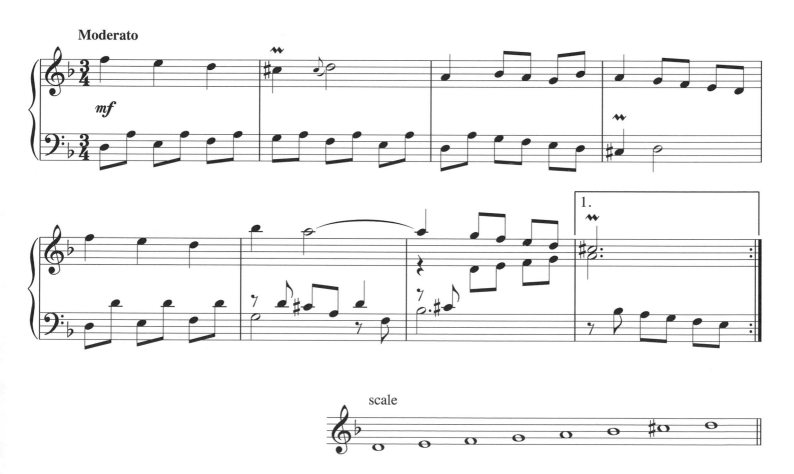

As you can hear, scales provide the essential sound or emotive quality of a musical composition or phrase in its most compact form. In this way, it is helpful to remember that a scale is similar to an artist's color palette: Each type of scale provides a unique color that can be imparted to a song or improvisation. A few pages hence, you will learn how to form scales from musical passages.

Historical Context

Scales are at the heart of the Western European tradition, as well as many other musical cultures. Compare these two examples—an ancient Greek melody and a Native American song. It is interesting to note that both utilize similar pitch content.

Song of Seikilos (100 B.C.–A.D. 100)

Serenade Song, *K'ilowawia*

How Scales Are Used

Before we delve into the theoretical details of scales, it will be helpful to consider how they are used. Although scales are often thought of as a mundane aspect of musicianship associated with developing technique, they are incredibly useful: scales can be used to analyze music to get in the mind of a composer or as the basis for a composition or improvisation. Fluency with scales not only helps with technique on an instrument, but also contributes to improved sight reading and facilitates chord spelling and interval identification. Arrangers and orchestrators frequently rely on scales for techniques such as planing, when multiple instruments move in parallel motion, and transposition. In short, scales are one of the most useful musical building blocks.

UNIT 2: BUILDING BLOCKS

Fortunately, the theory behind musical scales is one of the easiest aspects of theory to explore and to master. All that is required is to be able to differentiate between half steps and whole steps—the fundamental intervals in the Western European tradition.

Half Steps

The easiest way to understand half steps and whole steps is to visualize a piano keyboard like the one below.

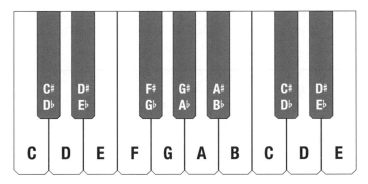

The important thing to remember is that *any* adjacent keys form a half step (also called a *semitone*). For example, a half step is formed between the notes C and C♯ (adjacent white and black notes) and a half step is also formed between B and C (adjacent white notes). The keyboard below shows several semitones.

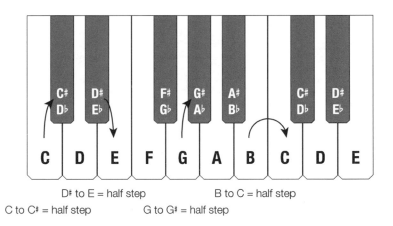

To ensure this concept is comfortable, complete the exercise below prior to moving on. Although scales are usually spelled with consecutive letter names (e.g., F–G–A–B), feel free to use any *enharmonic spellings* such as G♯/A♭ in your response. The answers are given in on page 51.

What note is a half step *above* B? _____

What note is a half step *below* E♭? _____

What note is a half step *above* F? _____

What note is a half step *below* A? _____

What note is a half step *above* D♭? _____

What note is a half step *below* F♭? _____

What note is a half step *above* C♭? _____

Did You Know?

Although the semitone is the fundamental building block of Western European music, this is not the case for other musical traditions. For example, jazz musicians frequently use notes called *blue notes* that fall between the half steps of a piano keyboard. Similarly, the Dhrupad tradition of North India divides an octave into 84 microtones! Even classical composers such as Haydn had a more nuanced ear for semitones than most musicians use today. For example, as Ross W. Duffin points out in *How Equal Temperament Ruined Harmony (and Why You Should Care)*, Haydn used the term *l'istesso tuono* in his manuscript for the String Quartet Op. 77/2 to indicate that pitch should not be altered when moving from the *enharmonic equivalent* E♭ to D♯, as would have been common in his day.

Whole Steps

Whole steps are similarly easy to find on a piano keyboard. Any two keys with a single key between them forms a whole step. Several whole steps are shown below: C to D, E to F♯, and A to B.

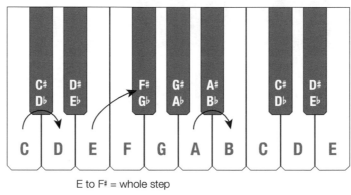

E to F♯ = whole step

C to D = whole step   A to B = whole step

Answer the following quiz. The answers are given on page 51.

What note is a whole-step *above* B? _____

What note is a whole-step *below* E♭? _____

What note is a whole-step *above* F? _____

What note is a whole-step *below* A? _____

What note is a whole-step *above* D♭? _____

What note is a whole-step *below* F♭? _____

What note is a whole-step *above* C♭? _____

UNIT 3: MAJOR SCALES

Major scales are one of the most common (and useful) scales found in classical music, pop, jazz, and other genres. The ubiquitous C major scale can be found by playing the white notes on a keyboard from C to C, or simply by writing consecutive musical letter names with no accidentals.

Although the notes of a scale can be used in any order in a composition or improvisation, scales are always written in ascending or descending letter-name order, as shown here:

It is interesting to note that most scales utilize all seven musical letter names, but this is not always the case. For example, a pentatonic scale contains five notes and an *octatonic* scale contains eight notes. (You will learn about those scales later in this book.)

Anatomy of a Major Scale

Major scales follow a specific pattern of whole steps and half steps. Instead of looking at the pattern of intervals for an entire scale, music theorists sometimes break scales into smaller segments. The term *tetrachord* is used to describe one such unit—a segment of four notes. It is interesting to note how a major scale is composed of two identical tetrachords with a whole step between.

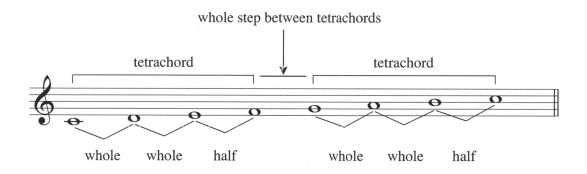

Another approach is to visualize a major scale as a combination of a *pentachord* (five-note segment) and a *tetrachord*:

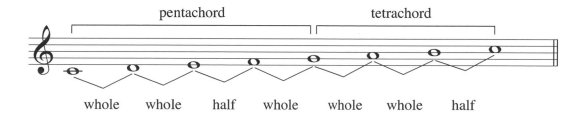

Although it may be helpful to visualize pentachords and tetrachords (using smaller segments may contribute to better accuracy), all major scales can also be visualized as the specific ordering of half steps and whole steps shown below:

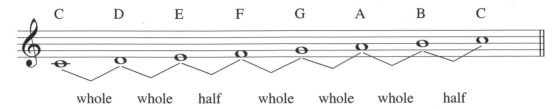

This pattern of whole and half steps (whole, whole, half; whole, whole, whole, half) forms a scale recipe that can be used to construct other major scales using a process called *transposition*. For example, a G major scale can be found by applying the same pattern to the starting note G:

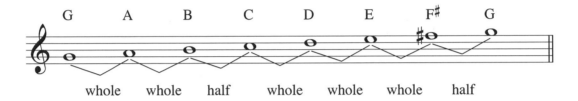

Note that in order to transpose a C major scale to the starting note G, an F♯ is required to maintain the same ordering of half steps and whole steps as the original scale.

Similarly, a D major scale can be constructed by applying the same pattern of whole steps and half steps to the starting note, D. Here, it is evident that an F♯ and C♯ are required to transpose the original scale to D.

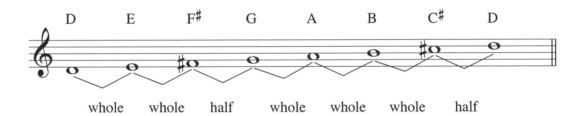

Use the major scale recipe (W–W–H, W–W–W–H) to spell the major scales given below. Remember that each major scale will be in letter-name order. For example, an A major scale contains the notes A–B–C♯, not A–B–D♭. It is interesting to note that an additional sharp will be required to complete each of these seven scales. The answers are given on page 51.

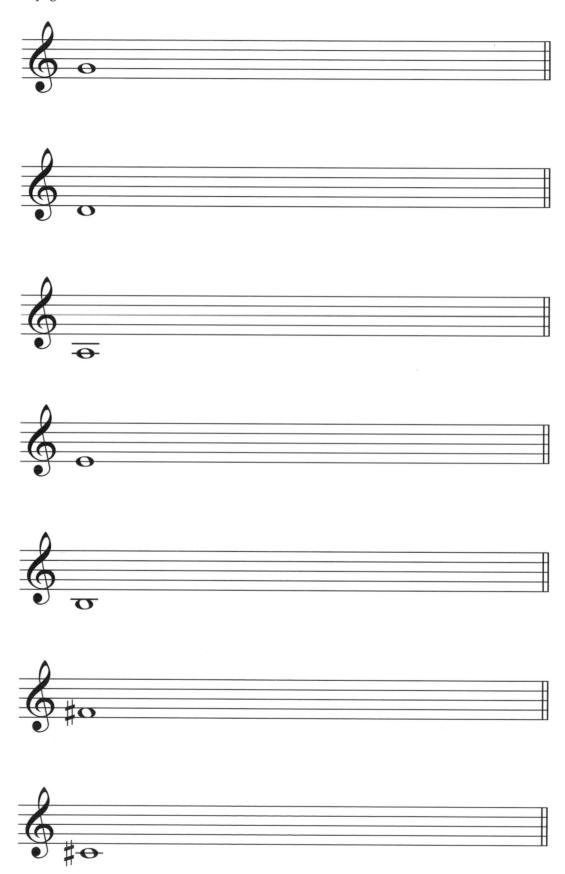

Use the major scale recipe (W–W–H, W–W–W–H) to spell the major scales listed below. In this case, an additional flat will be required to complete each scale. The answers are given on page 51.

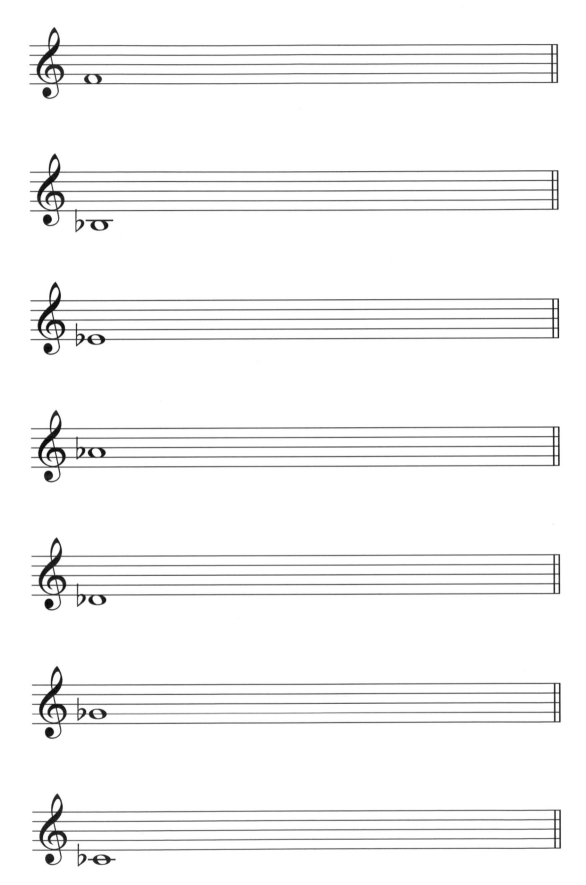

Circle of Fifths

The scales you have just constructed provide the basis for all the major *key signatures*—the sharps or flats typically found at the start of a composition that indicate the key upon which the composition is based. The relationship of keys can be seen in a common diagram called the *Circle of Fifths* (see below). The Circle of Fifths provides a helpful tool for visualizing (and memorizing) major scales and keys. Note that when proceeding clockwise around the circle, each key is five letter names (e.g., the interval of a fifth) higher the preceding key, hence the name Circle of Fifths. As you will learn in a moment, each key signature can imply two keys: a major and its relative minor.

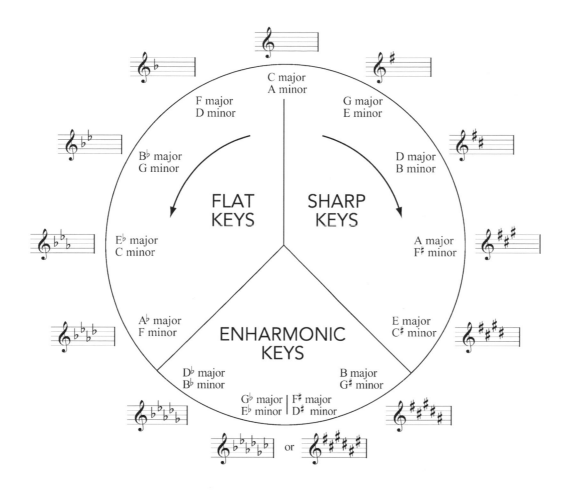

Tips for Memorizing the Circle of Fifths

It is cumbersome to construct major scales from whole steps and half steps, so most musicians use the Circle of Fifths to memorize the major key signatures. Rest assured that it is not unduly difficult (for example, it is much easier to memorize 12 keys than to memorize the multiplication table matrix), and you will be rewarded with a foundation that will enable you to easily play and spell all the scales in this book. Fluency with scales will also help you visualize intervals and chords. Here are a few tips that will make it easier to memorize the major key signatures:

- With the exception of F♯ and C♯, the first note of a sharp key is unaltered (e.g., C–G–D–A–E–B).
- With the exception of F major, all the flat keys start with a flat note (e.g., B♭, E♭, A♭, D♭, G♭, C♭).
- Count up five letters to find the next sharp key (e.g., C–G–D–A…).Count up four letters to find the next flat key (e.g., C–F–B♭–E♭…).
- Sharps are added to sharp keys in the following order: F♯, C♯, G♯, D♯, A♯, E♯, B♯. Repeat until memorized.
- Flats are added to flat keys in the following order: B♭, E♭, A♭, D♭, G♭, C♭, F♭. Repeat until memorized.

Scale Degree Terminology

By convention, musicians use special terms to describe each note of a scale. The terms provide a more nuanced way to refer to notes in a scale or key, and the terms imply an underlying function or tendency associated with each tone. Not only are the terms useful in identifying specific scale degrees, they are also used in the context of harmonic function. The scale degrees are shown below:

Tonic

For purposes of this book, the *tonic* is the first note of a scale, but the term also implies the note that is the most stable or the focal pitch of a composition. As you will see, the same collection of notes can be used to imply more than one tonic.

Supertonic

The *supertonic* is the note that is just above the tonic. Melodically, it is unstable and tends to want to move to the tonic or mediant.

Mediant

The *mediant* is midway between the tonic and the dominant. This tone is relatively stable.

Subdominant

The *subdominant* is the "dominant below." It is the fourth note of a given major scale and can also be found by counting down five letter names (or up four letter names) from the tonic. Melodically, the subdominant tends to sound highly unstable.

Dominant

As the name implies, the *dominant* is associated with a tone that is foundational in tonal music. Harmonically, dominant chords tend to resolve to tonic, but it is a relatively stable melodic tone.

Submediant

The *submediant* is the "mediant below," midway between the tonic and subdominant when placed below the tonic, and is the sixth scale degree of a given major scale. It can also be found by counting down three letters from the tonic.

Leading Tone

The *leading tone* is the seventh note of a major scale and is a half step below the tonic. It is the least stable tone to most listeners.

Scale Degree Identification

Applying terms such as tonic and mediant to other major scales, as well as other categories of scales, is easy if you remember the terms as they occur in a C major scale. The tonic is always the first note of the scale, the supertonic is always the second note, and so on for the other scale degrees in letter order. As an example, the scale degrees for a B♭ major scale are given below.

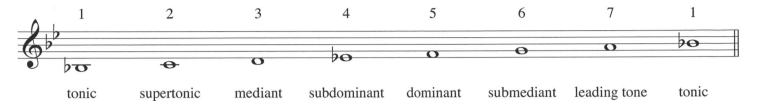

The following quiz will help you become more familiar with the association between notes and scales. The answers are given on page 52.

What note is the *supertonic* of an F major scale? _____

What note is the *dominant* of a D major scale? _____

What note is the *subdominant* of an E♭ major scale? _____

What note is the *mediant* in of a B major scale? _____

What note is the *leading tone* of a G major scale? _____

What note is the *submediant* of a D♭ major scale? _____

It is also helpful to turn the process around. For example, since we know that the supertonic is the second note in a major scale, it is possible to determine the scale that is associated with a given supertonic by counting *down* one letter name. Note that it is important to ensure that the given note is actually found in the key. In the example below, B♭ is the second note in A♭ major, *not* A major. As long as you check that the note is found in the given scale or key, letter-name counting is a good method for determining scale degrees such as supertonic, dominant, and mediant:

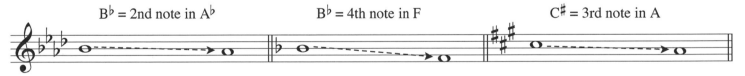

Although it is more common to associate a scale-degree terminology with a given major scale, the following quiz will help you develop fluency identifying scales in which specific notes are found. The answers are given on page 52.

The note E is the *supertonic* in which major scale? _____

The note A is the *dominant* in which major scale? _____

The note B♭ is the *subdominant* in which major scale? _____

The note F♯ is the *submediant* in which major scale? _____

The note E♭ is the *mediant* in which major scale? _____

The note G♯ is the *leading tone* in which major scale? _____

UNIT 4: MINOR SCALES

One of the interesting things about scales is that more than one tonic can be implied *with the same collection of notes.* You can explore this concept by improvising at the piano. Hold (or repeat) an A in the left hand and improvise using a C major scale in the right hand; you will notice that the A quickly establishes itself as the tonic (or "home") of the key. I always find it intriguing how the normally joyous sound of a major scale takes on a more melancholic effect simply by using the *same* notes in a different way.

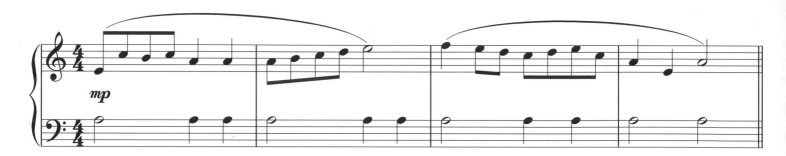

The relationship between a major scale and the submediant (scale degree six) is an important one that has been explored by composers for centuries. This relationship is so important that musicians use a specific term, *relative minor*, to describe how a given major key also contains a minor key. Count up to scale degree six (the submediant) to find the relative minor for a given major scale or key. Similarly, the *relative major* for a given minor key or scale can be found by counting down six tones (or up three tones) in the scale.

The examples below illustrate the process of finding the relative minor of several major scales/keys.

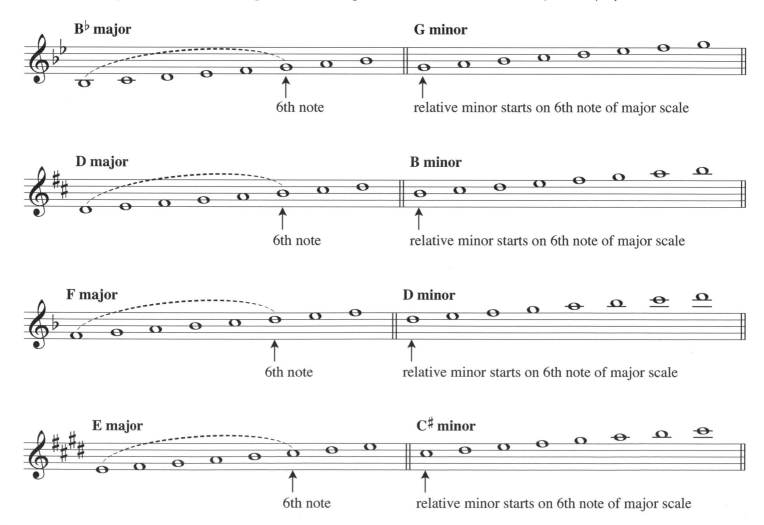

The questions below provide an opportunity to practice associating a major scale with its relative minor scale. Simply count up to the sixth note in the given scale—this will always yield the correct answer as long as you ensure that the note actually belongs to the given major scale. (The answers are given on page 52.)

The relative minor of D major is _____ minor.

The relative minor of F major is _____ minor.

The relative minor of E♭ major is _____ minor.

The relative minor of B major is _____ minor.

The relative minor of A major is _____ minor.

The relative minor of D♭ major is _____ minor.

Natural Minor

Musicians use the term *natural minor* to describe the minor scale that contains the same diatonic notes found in a given major key. For example, A minor is the relative minor of C major, and A minor is also the relative *natural minor* since the scale is unaltered by any chromatic notes outside of the key. Each of the minor scales in the preceding section are examples of natural minor scales.

Scale Degrees in Minor

When speaking of relative minor scales, it is important to note that scale degrees are moved to conform to the new tonic. For example, the note A is the *tonic* in A minor, the relative minor of C major, and the note C becomes the *mediant* in A minor. As is evident in the example below, one new term, *subtonic*, is used to describe the seventh note of a natural minor scale. This makes sense when you consider that the seventh note of a natural minor scale is a whole step below the tonic, so its tendency to want to resolve to the tonic is not as strong as a leading tone (which is only a half step away from the tonic).

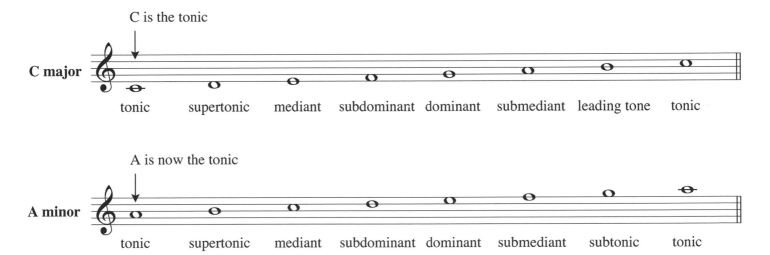

Several concepts are combined in the following exercise. Here, we find the relative minor by identifying scale degree six in the given major key. Then, we use the accidentals found in the major scale (or key signature) to write the natural minor form of the scale. Finally, we identify the given scale degree as it relates to the tonic of the minor scale. The first example has been completed. (The answers are given on page 52.)

F major

To find: mediant of relative minor of F major

F is the mediant in D minor

D major

To find: mediant of relative minor of D major

E♭ major

To find: subtonic of relative minor of E♭ major

G major

To find: subdominant of relative minor of G major

E major

To find: dominant of relative minor of E major

Harmonic Minor

Although the natural minor scale is the easiest one to write, the natural form of the scale is less common than the harmonic and melodic forms found in this section of the text. Composers and performers often utilize a leading tone instead of the subtonic and, as you can hear in the following example, the leading tone strengthens the movement to tonic, although the subtonic has a wonderfully quaint (or exotic) sound to most modern ears.

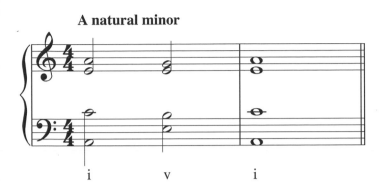

A natural minor

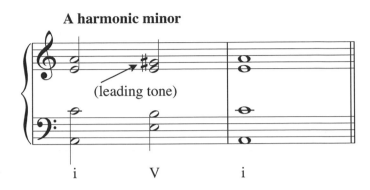

A harmonic minor

Adding a Leading Tone

Given that the leading tone is often used to strengthen a harmonic cadence—a point of harmonic rest—musicians refer to this form of a minor scale as the *harmonic minor* scale. To spell a harmonic minor scale, find the sixth note of a major scale and spell the natural form of the relative minor scale. Simply raise the seventh note, the subtonic, of the resulting natural minor scale a half step to form the harmonic version of the scale:

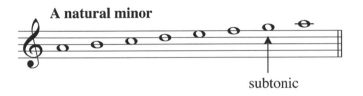

A natural minor

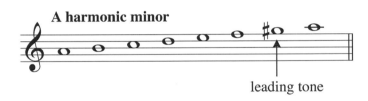

A harmonic minor

The process shown above can be applied to any other natural minor scale. Complete the following exercise to solidify this concept. The first one has been done for you. (The answers are given on page 53.)

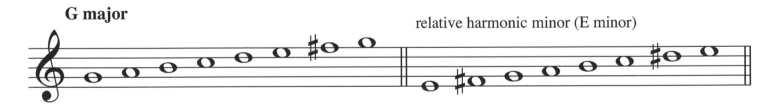

G major   relative harmonic minor (E minor)

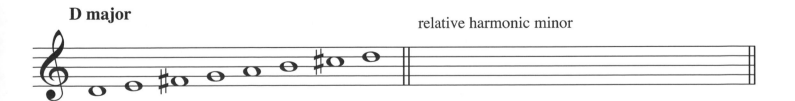

D major   relative harmonic minor

E♭ major relative harmonic minor

A♭ major relative harmonic minor

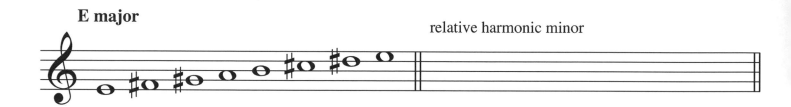

E major relative harmonic minor

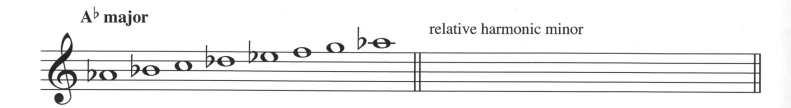

Melodic Minor

Another common form of minor scale is the *melodic minor*, a scale that derives its name from the fact that the sixth and seventh degrees of the scale are often raised in ascending melodic passages, such as the one below:

The process of writing or playing a melodic minor scale is similar to the way harmonic minor scales are formed: Find the sixth note of a major scale to identify the tonic of the relative minor and write the natural form of the scale using the same sharps or flats found in its relative major. Then, simply raise the sixth *and* seventh notes a half step to turn the natural minor scale into a melodic minor scale.

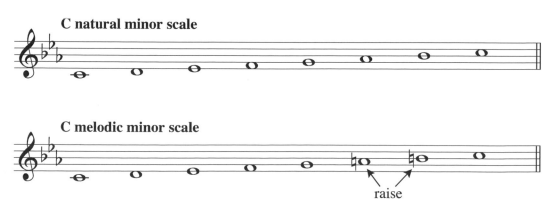

Melodic Minor Trick

One helpful tip that can be gleaned from the preceding example is that, other than the mediant, a melodic minor scale contains the same notes as a major scale sharing the same root. For example, C major contains no accidentals, and C melodic minor contains a single alteration—E♭, a lowered mediant. It is important to emphasize that this trick involves *parallel major* and *minor*, major and minor scales that share the same tonic, not *relative major* and *minor* as in the preceding examples. However, the trick makes it easy to find the ascending form of any melodic minor scale.

Melodic Minor: Descending

By convention, melodic minor scales return to the natural minor form in descent (see below). This makes sense when you try to sing the scale. Although it is comfortable to sing the raised sixth and seventh degrees of an ascending melodic minor scale, it is awkward to sing the same notes for a descending melodic passage. That is not to say the raised sixth and seventh are never found in descent; jazz musicians, in particular, frequently use the raised sixth and seventh in ascent and descent. Rather, it is a tendency that has evolved in the classical tradition.

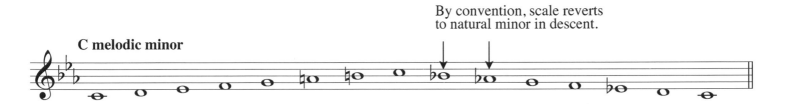

To internalize the concepts in this unit, complete the exercises that follow. Construct the melodic minor scales, as indicated. The first one has been done for you. (The answers are given on page 53.)

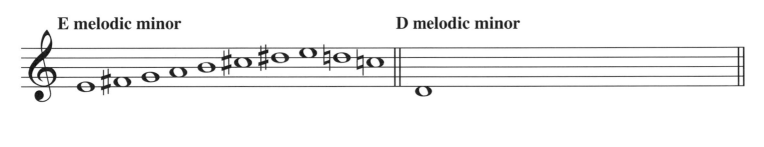

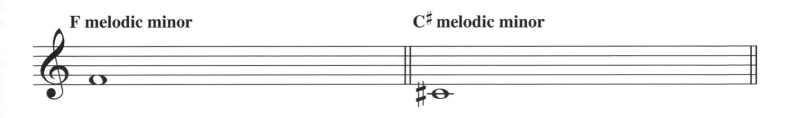

This exercise features all three forms of the relative minor scale—natural, harmonic, and melodic. Remember that the natural minor uses the same accidentals as its relative major. In contrast, the seventh degree of the scale is raised one half step to form the harmonic minor scale; the sixth *and* seventh degrees are raised to form the melodic minor scale. (The answers are given on page 53.)

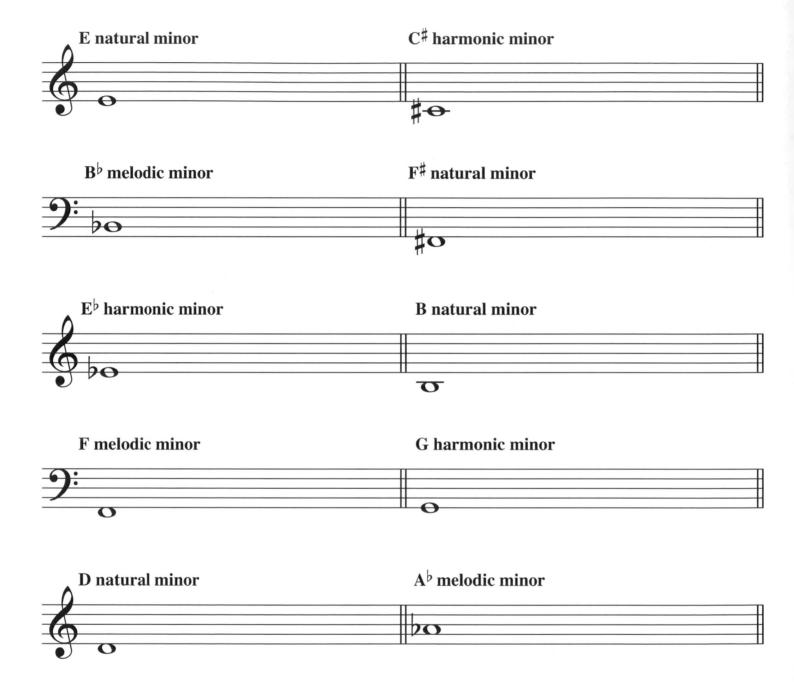

E natural minor

C# harmonic minor

B♭ melodic minor

F# natural minor

E♭ harmonic minor

B natural minor

F melodic minor

G harmonic minor

D natural minor

A♭ melodic minor

Minor Scales in the Real World

Composers sometimes mix natural, harmonic, and melodic minor scales. For example, the following chorale harmonization by J.S. Bach features all three forms of the A minor scale.

Herr, ich habe mißgehandelt

Differentiating Between Major and Minor

Given that relative minor and major scales share the same notes, how is it possible to differentiate between C major and A minor? That is a good question, but it's sometimes difficult to answer. In most cases, though, the tonic will be easy to identify by considering some or all of the following criteria:

- Compositions often start with the tonic.
- Compositions often end on the tonic.
- The tonic usually predominates: e.g., you would expect to see the note A emphasized in A minor.
- It is usually possible to identify the tonic aurally; the tonic will sound more stable than other tones.
- Accidentals outside the key or scale are evident when the harmonic or melodic forms of the minor scale are used.

Analysis: Major and Minor

It is sometimes helpful to analyze a passage of music to see if a composer utilized a specific scale. Although not all music will conform to a scale, the following steps will help you see if a particular scale was used as the basis for a musical passage. Let's look at another of Bach's chorale harmonizations.

Es stehn vor Gottes Throne

1. Identify the tonic by listening to the composition or looking for the clues listed in the previous section.

The note G predominantes throughout, including the start and end of the excerpt.

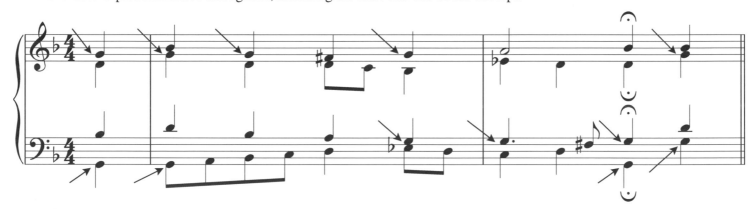

2. Starting with the tonic, form a scale by writing each note name (if found) in ascending letter-name order. Place a question mark above the staff for any missing letter names.

3. Look for accidentals or patterns of whole steps and half steps that would indicate a particular scale. Although it might be challenging to identify that a harmonic minor scale was used as the basis for the chorale excerpt, reordering the notes in ascending form made it possible to identify the scale, thus gaining an insight into the construction of the piece. As you will see in later sections of this book, the same process can be used to identify other scales.

Gm:

The key signature of B♭/Gm is implied by the two flats in this passage.

UNIT 5: PENTATONIC SCALES

As the name implies, a pentatonic scale is a scale with five notes. Although any five-tone scale can be described as *pentatonic*, there are two common forms of the scale that we will explore in this unit.

Creating a Major Pentatonic Scale

In Unit 3 we described how the subdominant (fourth note) and leading tone (seventh note) are particularly unstable tones. What happens if you remove those unstable tones from a scale? The result is the most common form of the pentatonic scale:

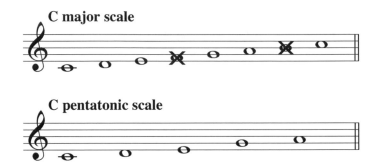

Be sure to play the scale several times on the piano (or another instrument) to get a sense of its unique sound. To my ear, the scale is calm and relaxing because of the absence of the two strong tendency tones. That might be one reason the scale shows up in so many cultures. The following African-American spiritual is one of countless tunes that utilize a pentatonic scale.

African-American Spiritual

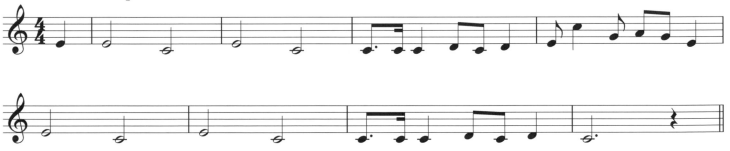

Exploring the Piano

The black notes on the piano happen to form a pentatonic scale, so it is an easy scale for non-pianists (and even non-musicians) to explore. "Pentatonic Dream" utilizes notes from a G♭ pentatonic scale.

Pentatonic Dream

Writing Pentatonic Scales

Write the following major scales (or use major key signatures if you have memorized them) and then cross out scale degrees 4 and 7 to form a major pentatonic scale. Alternatively, use a pentatonic "recipe" to construct each scale from scratch. The order of whole and half steps for a major pentatonic scale is: whole, whole, whole + half, whole. (The answers are given on page 54.)

Write the following pentatonic scales:

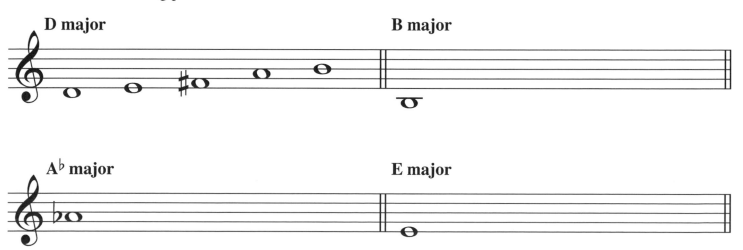

D♭ major   **F major**

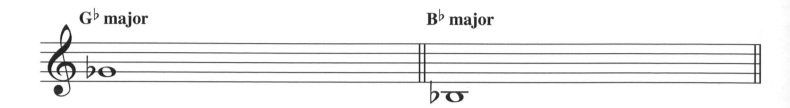

G♭ major   **B♭ major**

Minor Pentatonic Scales

In my experience, the most common form of *minor pentatonic* consists of a *major pentatonic* superimposed over its relative minor. In the example below, for instance, the notes of a C pentatonic scale are superimposed over A minor, the relative minor.

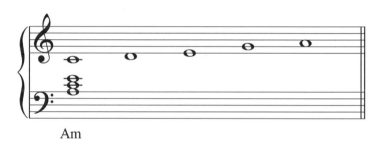

Am

The minor pentatonic scale can be heard in a wide variety of music, from Debussy to jazz and blues as well as many types of folk music from around the world. The following excerpt illustrates one approach taken by Chick Corea on his solo on "Steps" from the *Now He Sings, Now He Sobs* album.

Complete the following exercise to familiarize yourself with the most common form of the minor pentatonic scale. As with the last exercise, you can use the recipe for a minor pentatonic (whole + half, whole, whole, whole + half) or you can write a relative major scale and remove the fourth and seventh scale degrees (of the relative major scale) to form a minor pentatonic. The D minor pentatonic scale has been done for you. (The answers are given on page 54.)

Write the following minor pentatonic scales:

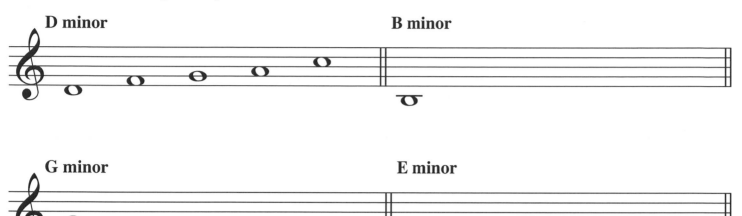

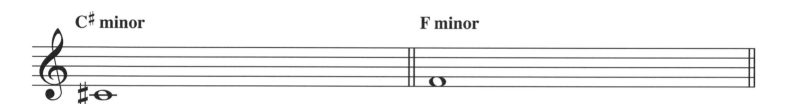

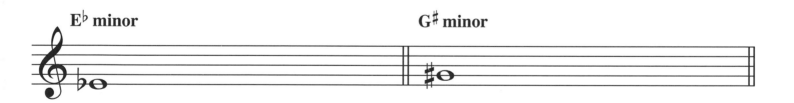

Other Forms of Minor Pentatonic Scale

Although less common, another form of minor pentatonic scale involves removing the fourth and seventh notes from a natural or melodic minor scale:

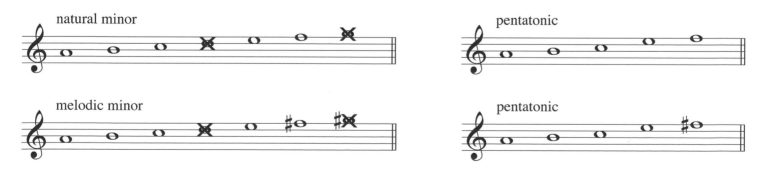

Both forms of the scale are interesting and have an effect that might be described as exotic.

Other Pentatonic Scales

Although the most common forms of pentatonic scales consist of the major and minor pentatonic, any number of interesting scales can be formed with just five notes. Interestingly, even though each of the scales in this section sounds unique, they all seem to retain an underlying pentatonic quality that can be identified aurally.

One way to explore new forms of the scale is to write a diatonic pentatonic scale consisting of the notes C–D–E–G–A. Next, consider applying accidentals to some of the notes. For example, the notes C–D♭–E–G–A♭ sound exotic, while the scale consisting of the notes C–D–E–G–A♭ might be considered more subtle. You can also explore other letter names, such as a consecutive pattern of notes, to yield many interesting variants. Here are a few:

UNIT 6: MODES

The term *mode* (also *Gregorian mode* or *church mode*) is used to describe a fascinating category of scales that have been around for hundreds of years. Not only were modes utilized by composers of early church music, they have been employed by many jazz and popular musicians, including Miles Davis, McCoy Tyner, and Carlos Santana, as well as by composers of 20th century art music. Modes are also frequently heard in feature films. In short, modes are one of the most useful categories of scales.

What Is a Mode?

In a previous unit you learned that the notes of a major scale can be used to imply a minor scale. For example, if you improvise on the white notes of the piano (C major) but focus on the note A, the A will quickly establish itself as a tonic and an A minor tonality will emerge. Interestingly, *any* of the seven notes of a major scale can function as a tonic if the note is emphasized harmonically or melodically. The following melodies demonstrate this concept. In these examples, several different tonic notes are implied by the same major scale. Be sure to play or sing the examples to hear how notes other than C can emerge as a new tonic.

Take time to explore the following modal improvisation exercise in order to internalize this concept:

1. Select a major scale.
2. Pick a note that you want to establish as the tonic.
3. Play (or sing) the new tonic several times.
4. Improvise and emphasize the tonic triad (consisting of scale degrees 1, 3, and 5).
5. Improvise using other notes in the scale, but return to the tonic triad as needed to establish the mode.

Mode Names

Musicians use specific terms to describe each of the modes of a major scale. The terms, which are of Greek origin, were obfuscated by medieval scholars, but today we still use the terms shown below. (Note that scholars of early music use a more complex modal taxonomy that includes terms such as *Hypodorian* and *Hypophrygian*. The terms are rarely used outside of academe, so we will limit the discussion to the common categories listed here.)

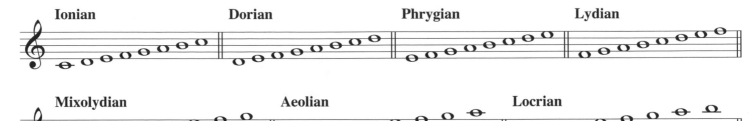

The important thing to remember about modes is that the names of the modes are not just a fancy term for the scale degrees. Each mode has a distinctive sound or color, so terms such as Lydian or Dorian imply a specific emotive effect.

Internalizing the Sound of Each Mode

One way to familiarize your ear with the sound or emotive quality of each mode is to use your left hand to play an *ostinato*—a repeating pattern—at the piano while you improvise with the right hand. An example is given here.

Phrygian Improvisation

Note that you do not need to know how to play piano to explore modes in this way. You could even use the index finger of each hand to explore modes, using the following steps:

1. Select a key you wish to explore and choose a new tonic representing the mode you intend to imply.

2. Use the tonic of the mode as the bottom note of a left-hand ostinato. In this way, the left hand will establish a clear tonal center.

3. Improvise a melody in the right hand and explore the emotive effect of the mode.

4. Repeat for other modes.

Mode-Writing Tips

Many students learn to write and identify modes by memorizing the pattern of whole steps and half steps for each of the seven modes. Although it is possible to learn modes in this way, and the process works well for some modes, including Lydian and Mixolydian, memorizing multiple whole- and half-step patterns can be cumbersome and error-prone. My advice is to learn the modes in the key of C and apply the terms to other keys. For example, we know that D Dorian is the second mode of C major. Thus, if you are asked to write or play an A Dorian scale, simply ask yourself, "What is the major scale or key that has an A as the second note of the scale?" It is not hard to determine that A is the second note of a G major scale.

Similarly, if you are asked to write or play a B♭ Mixolydian scale, start by visualizing a Mixolydian scale in the key of C. As you already learned, G is the Mixolydian (fifth) mode of C. Hence, you need only determine the major scale that contains B♭ as its fifth note to identify the notes that are found in a B♭ Mixolydian scale: B♭ is the fifth mode of E♭ major; thus, the three flats found in E♭ major provide the necessary accidentals to spell a B♭ Mixolydian scale.

Another, somewhat slower, approach is to use the order of whole steps and half steps found in a major scale and adjust the start of the pattern to correspond to the start of the mode. For example, as you learned in the first unit, the pattern for a major scale is W–W–H–W–W–W–H. To write a Dorian mode for an arbitrary tonic note, simply start the pattern on the second note (W–H–W–W–W–H–W). Similarly, the pattern for the Phrygian mode is (starting on the third note of the major-scale pattern) H–W–W–W–H–W–W.

Write the following modes, using your method of choice. The D Lydian mode has been completed for you. (The answers are given on page 54.)

Write the following modes:

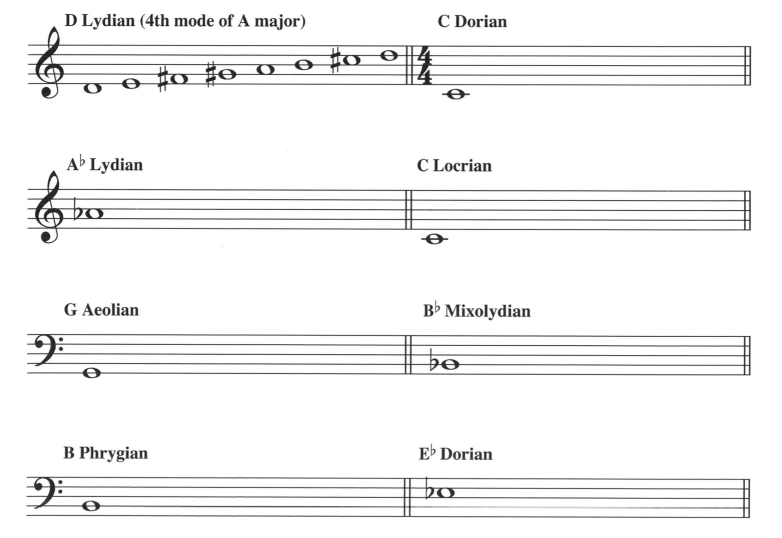

Comparing Modes That Share the Same Tonic

For the sake of comparison, it is interesting to construct all seven modes starting with the same tonic note. As is evident below, it is the unique combination of whole steps and half steps that provides the distinctive sound of each mode.

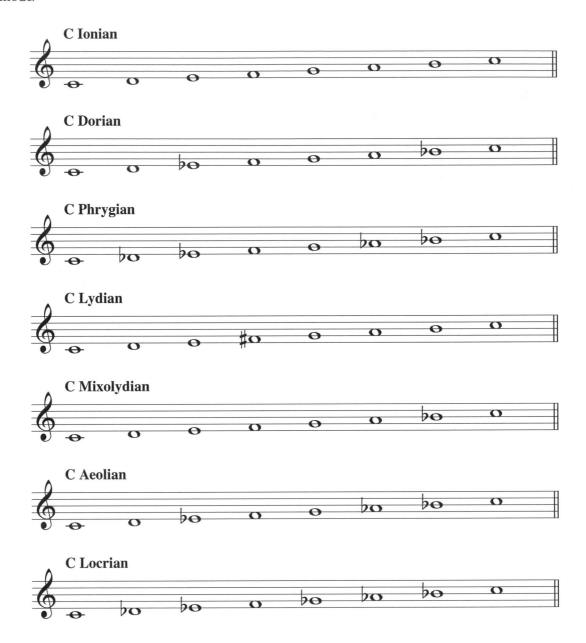

Analyzing Modal Music

One of the things I love about analysis is that it helps me in my work as a composer and improviser by providing a deeper understanding of music. Hence, the process of identifying a scale or mode upon which a composition has been based can yield interesting insights. The method for recognizing a mode is similar to the procedure for determining a major scale:

1. Select a starting note and write it on a blank staff. You can use any arbitrary tone in the composition or select the note that you think might be the tonic.

2. Look for each of the other letter names and write them, in ascending order, on the staff. Write a question mark for any missing notes. This will help you visualize modes in which a missing note *could* be natural, sharp, or flat as needed to correspond to a given mode or key signature.

3. See if the scale corresponds to one of the major scales shown in Unit 1. If it does, the composition is either major, natural minor, or modal. If the notes do not correspond with a major scale, it would indicate that

the scale might be harmonic or melodic minor or one of the scales shown later in the book. Note that not all compositions fit a particular scale or modality.

4. Assuming the scale corresponds with one of the major scales, identify the tonic by playing the example or looking for other clues that might indicate the tonic, such as looking at the first and last note and considering any notes that seem to be emphasized throughout the piece.

5. Rewrite the scale starting with the tonic note. The mode is named by the tonic note and its relationship to the major scale found in step three.

The following melody demonstrates how the previous steps could be applied to a modal composition or excerpt.

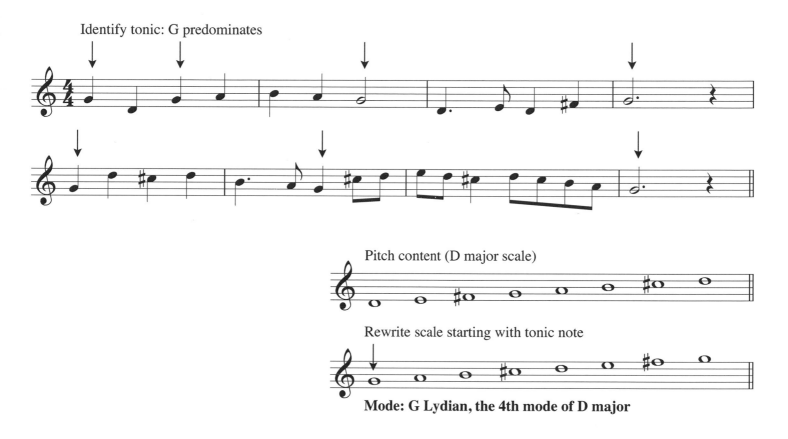

Identify tonic: G predominates

Pitch content (D major scale)

Rewrite scale starting with tonic note

Mode: G Lydian, the 4th mode of D major

Use the steps illustrated in the previous section to analyze the modal melodies below. (The answers are given on page 54.)

mode: _____

mode: _____

mode: _____

UNIT 7: COMMON SCALES IN JAZZ AND POPULAR MUSIC

Scales are an important foundation of classical music, but they are also useful in popular styles, including jazz, rock, country, and pop. In this section we will look at some of the most useful scales employed by composers and improvisers in popular idioms.

Blues Scales

The blues scale is often one of the first scales learned by budding improvisers. Although it is less common to hear the blues scale performed in its scalar form on recordings, the palette of notes contained in the blues scale is frequently heard on recordings. The musical examples below show the notes of a C blues scale and an excerpt from an improvised solo by Oscar Peterson.

Solo excerpt from "Between the Devil and the Deep Blue Sea"
(transposed to C)

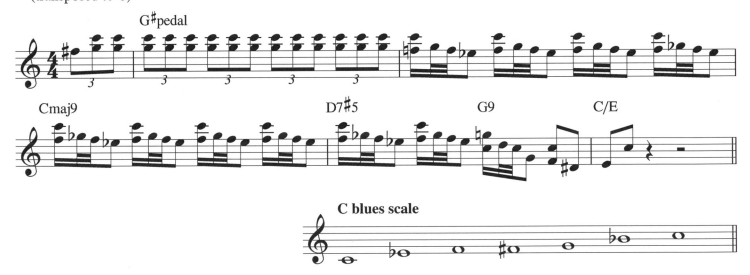

Writing and Playing Blues Scales

One way to visualize a blues scale is as a minor pentatonic scale with a passing tone. As you may recall from the last section, a minor pentatonic can be visualized as a pentatonic based on the relative major. Thus, an E♭ major pentatonic provides almost all the notes for a C blues scale. In the figure below, a passing tone (F♯) is added between the F and G to form a blues scale.

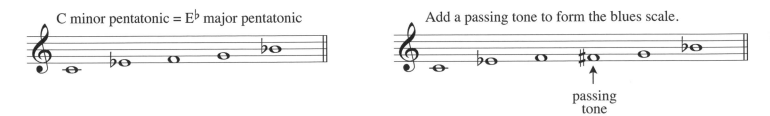

Writing or playing blues scales in other keys is just as easy:

1. Find the pentatonic a step and a half higher than the given chord or key.
2. Add a passing tone between the second and third notes of the pentatonic (or scale degrees four and five of the key, depending on the way you prefer to visualize it).

Writing Exercise: Blues Scales

Use the steps outlined in the previous paragraph to write blues scales listed below. Note that these scales work well for major and minor chords (e.g., C7 or Cm7). The F blues scale has been done for you. (The answers are given on page 55.)

Write the following blues scales:

F blues   **G blues**

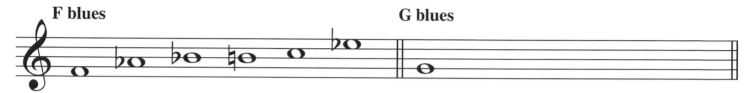

B blues   **E♭ blues**

A blues   **E blues**

F♯ blues   **B♭ blues**

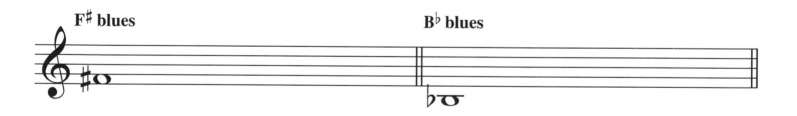

Demonstration Composition: Blues Shoes

"Blues Shoes" demonstrates how a blues scale might be used as the basis for a composition or improvisation. Be sure to listen to blues recordings to get a feel for the style as well as additional insights regarding how the scale is used "in the wild." A few of my favorite artists who utilize blues vocabulary include Oscar Peterson, Stevie Ray Vaughan, Jimmy Smith, and Horace Silver.

Blues Shoes

Three Applications of a Major Scale

Most improvisers and composers understand the close relationship that exists between chords and scales. In this section we will look at three of the most common chord and scale relationships, but bear in mind that a given major scale will typically sound good over *any* of the chords that are derived from the scale.

Conceptualizing Chord and Scale Relationships

The ii–V–I progression might be described as a "building block" progression in jazz and some forms of popular music. (For a given key, the Roman numerals ii–V–I are used to indicate chords that are built on the supertonic, dominant, and tonic, respectively.) Many songs, including "Satin Doll," "Alone Together," "How High the Moon," and "I'll Remember April" consist primarily of a series of ii–V–I progressions in various keys. The example that follows illustrates how the harmonic motion from the first part of "How High the Moon" consists of a tonic chord followed by ii–V–I progressions in the temporary keys of F major and E♭ major.

How High the Moon

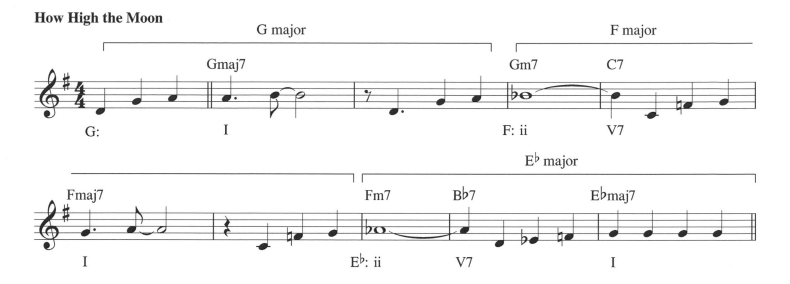

Given how common ii–V–I progressions are, when improvising, it is helpful to recognize that the same scale can be used as a compositional or improvisational palette for three common chord categories: minor 7th, dominant 7th, and major 7th. (This also works for any *extended* variation, such as adding a 9th or 13th.)

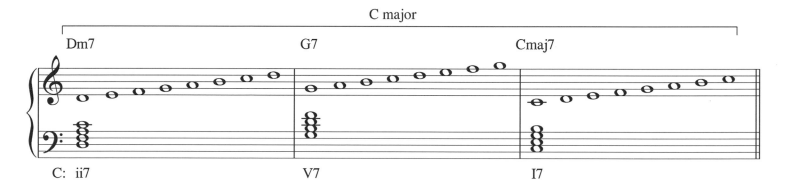

Recognizing ii–V–I progressions

One way to apply a major scale is to look for ii–V–I progressions in various keys. Major ii–V–I progressions follow a predictable pattern of min7–V7–maj7, with or without extensions such as 9 or 13, and the root movement of the progression is descending fifths:

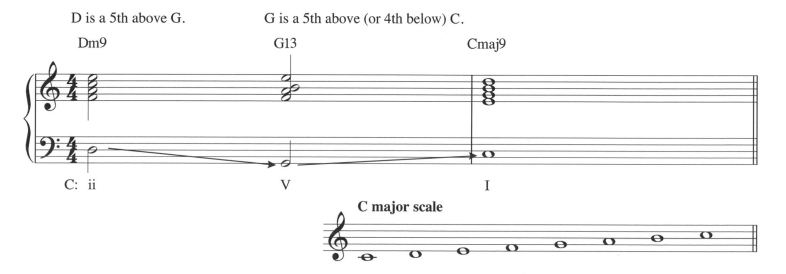

Three Common Applications of a Major Scale

Applying major scales based on harmonic function may be challenging to players who do not have a background in harmony, so it may be more helpful to consider chord and scale relationships on a chord-by-chord basis. This sort of approach is also helpful for navigating harmonic progressions that do not follow a predictable pattern. The following tips will be useful in constructing scales for three of the most common categories of chords.

Chord	Tip	Example
Minor 7th	Major scale down one whole step from root (same notes as a Dorian scale sharing the same tonic as the chord root)	Use F major scale for Gm7 (same notes as G Dorian)
Dominant 7th	Major scale with lowered seventh (this is the same as a Mixolydian scale sharing the same root)	C Mixolydian scale for C7
Major 7th	Major scale sharing the same root as the given chord	D major scale for Dmaj7 chord

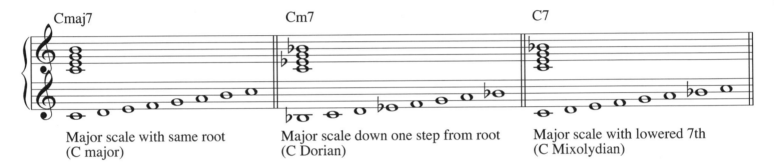

Cmaj7 — Major scale with same root (C major)

Cm7 — Major scale down one step from root (C Dorian)

C7 — Major scale with lowered 7th (C Mixolydian)

Writing Exercise

Although each of the scales in the previous section can be visualized as a mode, I have noticed that it is often easier to picture these as a major scale with an alteration. For example, it is easy to turn a concert B♭ scale into a B♭ Mixolydian scale by lowering the seventh note (A) to A♭. Similarly, the notes of a Dorian scale can be quickly found by envisioning a major scale down a whole step (E♭ major for Fm7, or G major for Am7) or by lowering the third and seventh of a major scale. Use these tips to write an appropriate scale for each of the following chords. The first one has been done for you. (The answers are given on page 55.)

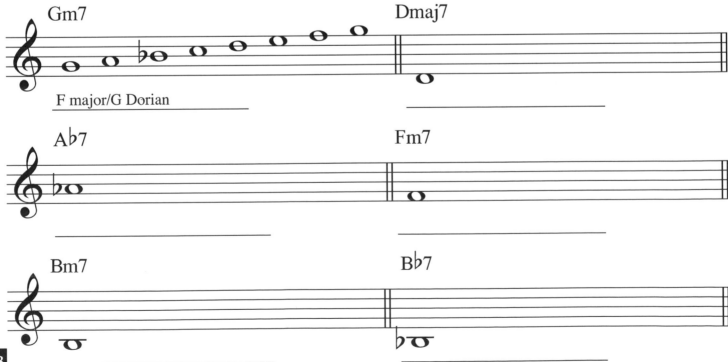

Gm7 — F major/G Dorian

Dmaj7

A♭7

Fm7

Bm7

B♭7

Demonstration Composition

The piece below illustrates how the tips in this section could be used as the basis for a composition or an improvisation. Note that, as with previous examples, the tones of the scales are not necessarily used in letter-name order in the composition.

Brightly, in one

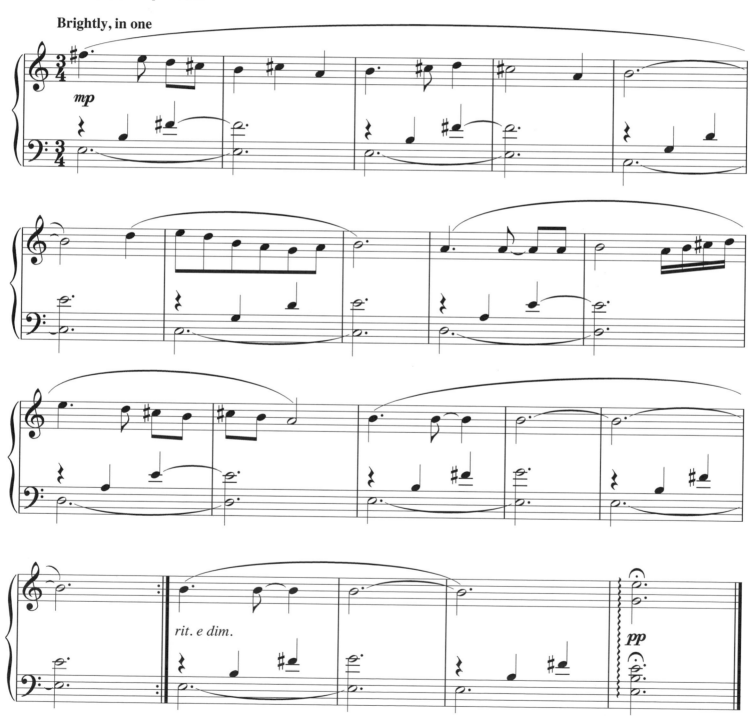

Four Applications of Melodic Minor Scale

Where major scales are a useful resource when applied to three common chords in jazz and popular music (minor 7th, dominant 7th, and major 7th), melodic minor scales are useful as an improvisational or compositional palette for four of the most challenging chord categories: half-diminished, altered, Lydian-dominant, and minor(maj7).

Review

As we mentioned in Unit 4, an easy way to visualize a melodic minor scale is to think of a major scale with a lowered third. When applying melodic minor scales in jazz and popular music, the scale (shown below) does not usually revert to the natural minor form in descent.

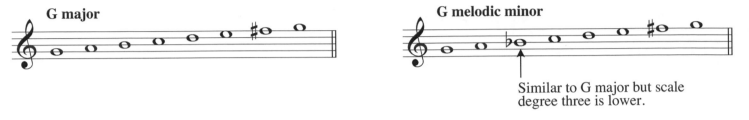

Similar to G major but scale degree three is lower.

Although the tips presented in this section might seem counterintuitive, it is helpful to remember that the scales are a linear representation of vertical chord structures. For example, a C melodic minor scale contains all the notes of a Cm(maj13) chord.

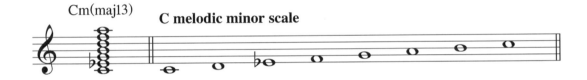

We won't delve into the intricacies of jazz and popular harmony in this book, so suffice it to say that each of the scales in this section represents a similar relationship between a scale and its related chord structure.

Tonic Minor

I use the term "tonic minor" to describe a category of minor chords that typically functions as a tonic in a given key: Cm6, Cm6/9, Cm(maj7), Cm(maj9), Cm(maj11), Cm(maj13). To determine a scale for a tonic minor chord, simply spell a melodic minor scale with the same root as the given minor chord. The C melodic minor scale is given as an example.

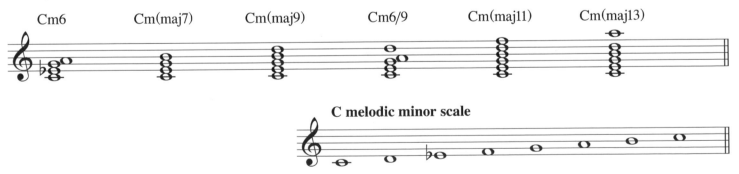

Half Diminished

Melodic minor scales can also be applied to half diminished chords (also described as m7♭5). In this instance, spell a melodic minor scale using the third of the chord as the root of the scale. The example below shows how a C melodic minor scale can be used over Am7♭5. As with the preceding example, the notes of the scale contain most of the chord tones, including the root, third, lowered fifth, seventh, and eleventh.

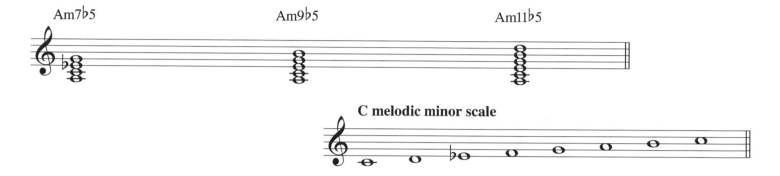

Altered Dominant

Altered dominant chords (V7 chord with alterations of the fifth or ninth) frequently precede a tonic. Interestingly, a melodic minor scale can be superimposed over the altered chord to provide all the primary chord tones and altered chord tones. As is evident in the example below, a melodic minor scale up one half step from the root of the chord contains the root, third, and seventh of the chord as well as the altered fifths and ninths. (Note that most of the tones in the scale are enharmonic equivalents for a given chord tone.)

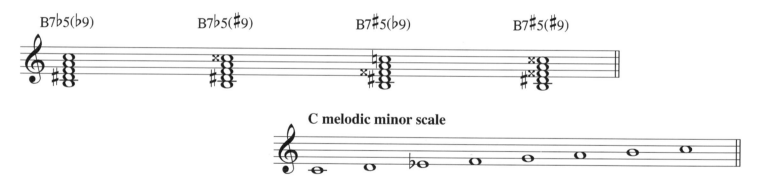

Lydian Dominant

A final application of the melodic minor scale involves the so called "Lydian dominant" chord—a major-minor seventh chord containing the raised eleventh ("Lydian" tone). Here, a melodic minor scale based on the fifth of the chord contains the root, third, seventh, raised eleventh, and extensions:

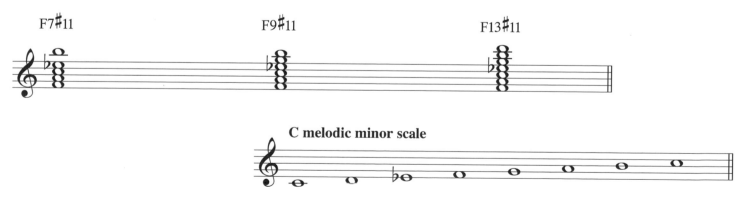

Review

Let's review the four common applications of a melodic minor scale. Notice how the same melodic minor scale can be used in four different ways, as shown in the following table:

Chord type	Tip	Example
Tonic minor	Use a melodic minor scale with the same root note as the given chord.	C melodic minor scale for Cm6, Cm(maj7), Cm(maj9), Cm(maj13), and Cm6/9
Half diminished	Spell a melodic minor starting on the third of the chord.	C melodic minor scale for Am7♭5, Am9♭5 , and Am11♭5
Altered dominant	Use a melodic minor scale up one half step from the root of the altered chord.	C melodic minor scale for B7alt., B7♯5(♭9), B7♭5(♯9), B7♭5(♯9), and B7♭5(♭9)
Lydian dominant	Use a melodic minor starting on the fifth of the chord.	C melodic minor scale for F7♯11, F9♯11, and F13♯11

Writing Exercise

Use the tips from the preceding section to write an appropriate melodic minor scale for each of the following chords. The first four examples have been completed for you. (The answers are given on page 55.)

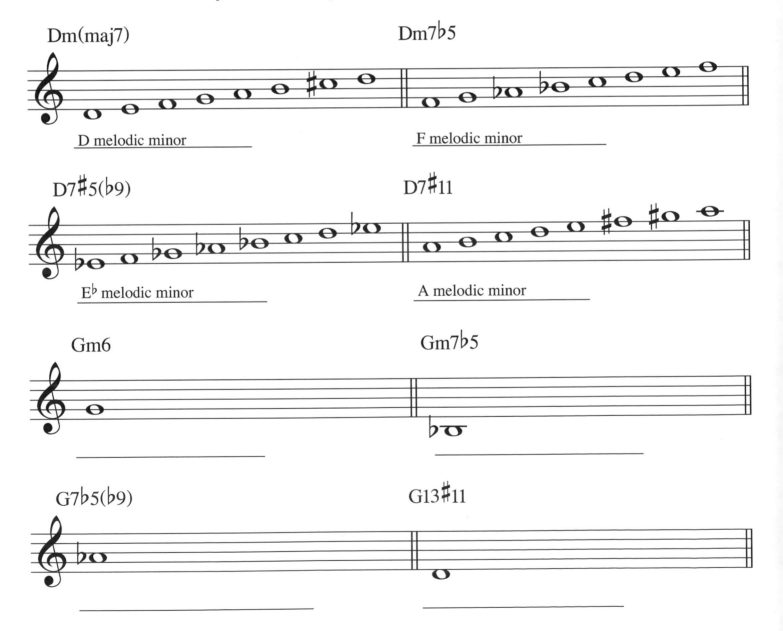

Dm(maj7) — D melodic minor

Dm7♭5 — F melodic minor

D7♯5(♭9) — E♭ melodic minor

D7♯11 — A melodic minor

Gm6

Gm7♭5

G7♭5(♭9)

G13♯11

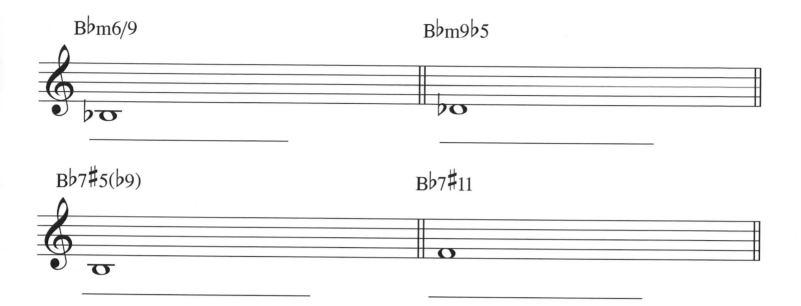

Bbm6/9

Bbm9b5

Bb7#5(b9)

Bb7#11

Analysis: Do Improvisers Really Think This Way?

Students sometimes question whether mature improvisers really use theory in their improvisations. My response is that theory can *inform* the creative process. Although it would be ludicrous to suggest that master musicians like Bill Evans or Kenny Barron rely solely on scales in their improvisations, analysis reveals that a knowledge of scales *does* inform their work. In the following excerpt from Kenny Barron's "Until Then," notice how most of the notes fit within expected chord and scale relationships, yet Barron uses the scale tones in an artistic way:

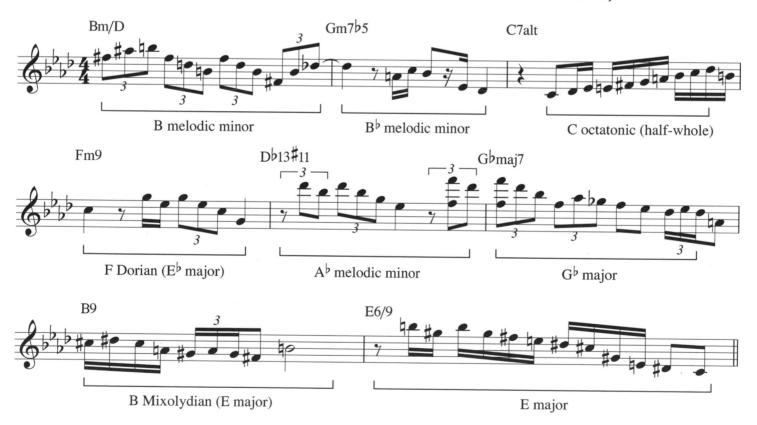

Looking ahead

Although many other scales are utilized by jazz and popular musicians, the scales presented in this unit represent the some of the most common chord and scale relationships. We will explore several other scales in Unit 8: Synthetic Scales.

UNIT 8: SYNTHETIC SCALES

Some music theorists use the term *synthetic scale* to describe a category of scales, created by modern composers, that are not major, minor, or a mode. In this unit we will look at a number of exotic scales that are interesting to use as composition or improvisation resources.

Symmetrical Scales

Symmetrical scales represent one category of synthetic scales consisting of a repeating interval or interval pattern such as whole step, whole step, whole step, or half step, whole step, half step, whole step.

Chromatic Scale

While the chromatic scale is not usually considered an exotic scale, it *is* an example of a symmetrical scale. As the name implies, a chromatic scale consists entirely of semitones. By convention, sharps are used in the ascending form and flats for the descending version of the scale:

Understanding the convention of using sharps for ascending chromatic passages and flats for descending chromatic passages can help you write music that will be easier for musicians to read. For example, notice how a careful use of accidentals clarifies the following passage:

Awkward: Accidentals are hard to read.   Better: Accidentals are easier to read.

One of my favorite chromatic passages can be heard in a composition from Sergei Prokofiev's *Visions Fugitives*. Notice how Prokofiev utilizes a chromatic scale to underscore a melody in the right hand:

Lentamente

In order to solidify the concept of ascending and descending chromatics, fill in the missing chromatic note in the following exercise. The answers are given on page 56.

1. Ascending:	A	A#	B	5. Ascending:	C	___	D
2. Descending:	G	___	F	6. Descending:	D	___	C
3. Ascending:	D	___	E	7. Ascending:	F	___	G
4. Descending:	B	___	A	8. Descending:	E	___	D

Whole Tone Scale

The whole tone scale consists solely of whole steps that divide the octave into six equal parts. The scale can be heard in the compositions of many 20th century composers, including Debussy and Bartók. It has what might be described as a magical or ethereal quality, as in Debussy's piano prelude *Voiles* ("Sails"):

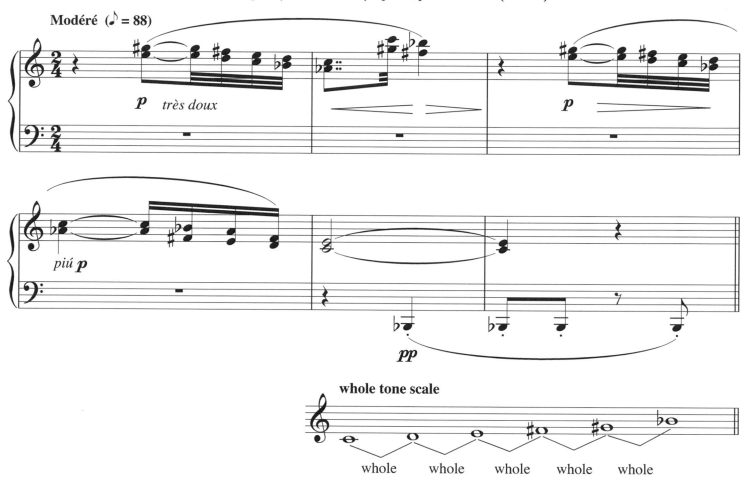

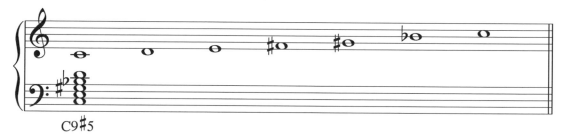

The whole tone scale can also be heard in jazz, likely through the influence of Debussy and Ravel on composers like Bix Beiderbecke. A common application is to superimpose a whole tone scale over a dominant seventh chord. This approach provides the root, third, seventh, and ninth, as well as a raised and lowered fifth:

C9#5

Octatonic/Diminished Scale

The octatonic scale, also known as the diminished scale, consists of alternating half and whole steps. The scale is unique in that it contains two diminished seventh chords. As the name implies, an octatonic scale contains eight notes. Note that several spellings are possible because one letter name must be used twice.

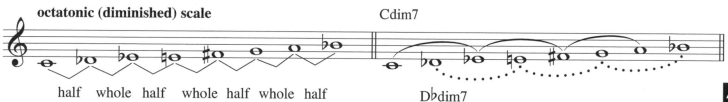

The octatonic scale has been utilized by a number of 20th century composers, including Debussy, Ravel, Stravinsky, and others. The following is an excerpt from from Béla Bartók's *Mikrokosmos*:

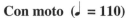

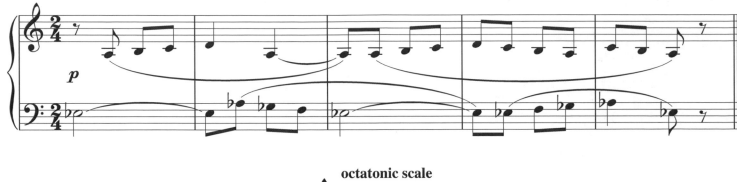

octatonic scale

The scale is also frequently employed by jazz artists in two common ways. In the first example, an alternating half- and whole-step scale is applied to an altered dominant chord. In the second example, an alternating whole- and half-step octatonic scale is used over a fully diminished seventh chord:

Alternating half steps and whole steps

Alternating whole steps and half steps

C13♭9

Cdim7

Writing Exercise: Synthetic Scales

Complete the following exercise before moving on. Note that more than one choice of accidental may be appropriate for these exercises since the scales do not conform to the traditional pattern of seven letter names found in non-synthetic scales. (The answers are given on page 56.)

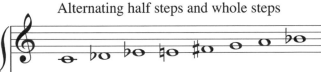

E octatonic (half/whole)

G whole tone

B♭ chromatic (descending)

E♭ whole tone

G octatonic (whole/half)

A chromatic (ascending)

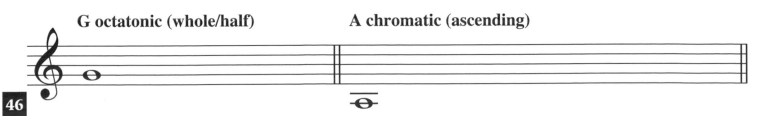

Demonstration Composition: Octatonic Mirage

One of the things I love about music theory is that it can open the door to innumerable creative applications, and symmetrical scales represent one such opportunity. "Octatonic Mirage" demonstrates one approach to utilizing an octatonic scale as a melodic and harmonic resource.

Octatonic Mirage

Analysis Tips

It can be challenging to analyze music that is built around symmetrical (or other synthetic) scales. As I mentioned in Unit 4, a good approach is to identify a tonic (if possible) and to write all the notes in ascending order. Because the accidentals of a synthetic scale will not align with traditional scales and key signatures, it is usually helpful to look at the interval relationships. Note how the pattern of alternating whole steps is evident in the following excerpt. This indicates that the composer utilized a whole tone scale.

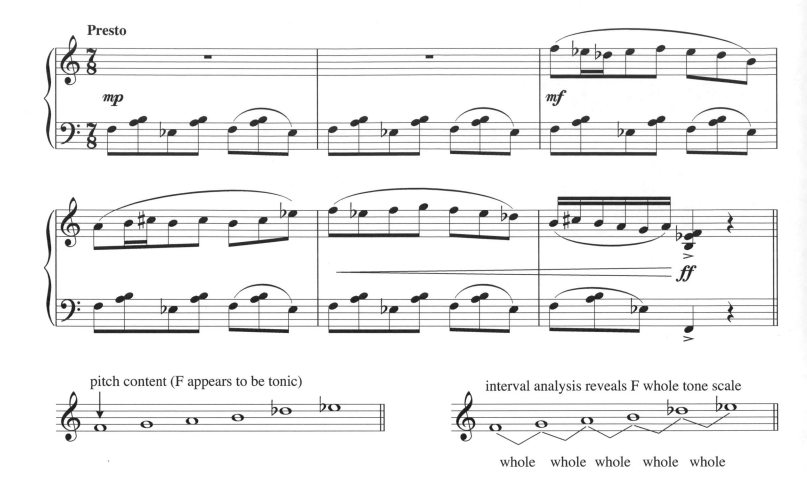

pitch content (F appears to be tonic)

interval analysis reveals F whole tone scale

whole   whole whole   whole   whole

Use the concepts you learned in this section to determine the scales upon which the following compositions were based. (The answers are given on page 56.)

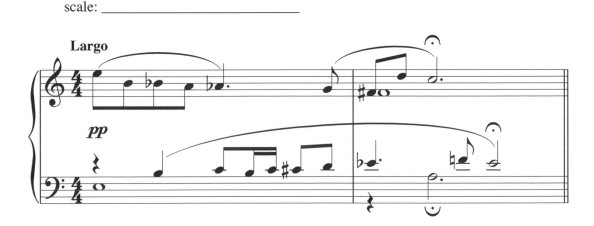

scale: _____

Largo

scale: _____

Other Synthetic Scale Formations

Although this book covers many of the common scales utilized by performers, composers, and improvisers, many other scales are feasible. Not only are there additional possibilities within the framework of the 12 semitones available to musicians in the Western European tradition, but a virtually unlimited number of workable options is at one's disposal when intervals other than half steps are up for grabs. The following chart, based on Vincent Persichetti's book, *Twentieth-Century Harmony*, demonstrates a number of interesting scale formations. A final exercise, which should provide many hours of exploration, is found at the bottom of the page.

Synthetic Scale Formations

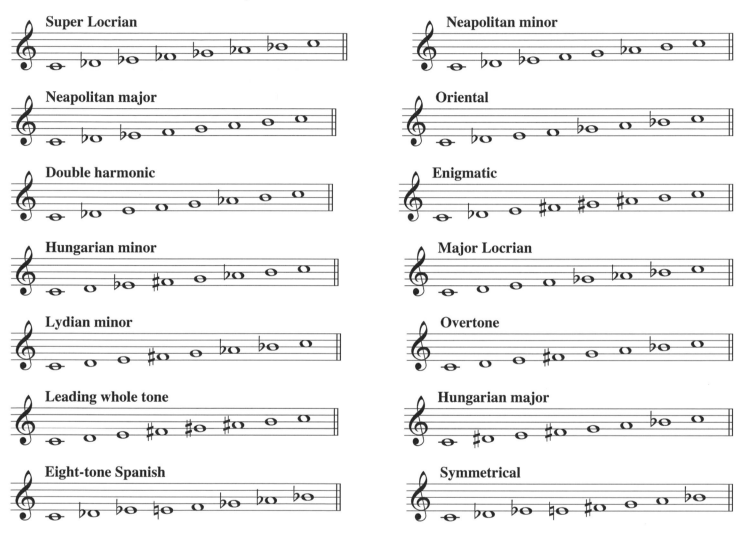

Exercise: Synthetic Scale Exploration

1. Select a scale from the synthetic formations given above.

2. At the piano, play the scale in the right hand over the tonic in the left.

3. Create a melodic improvisation in order to explore the unique sound of the scale.

4. Create triads consisting of alternate notes from the scale. For example, the tonic chord in Super Locrian is a C diminished triad (C–E♭–G♭) while the supertonic chord is a D♭m triad (D♭–F♭–A♭).

5. Explore the triadic harmonies of the scale.

6. Explore quartal and quintal harmonies, chords constructed from the interval of a fourth or fifth.

7. Combine melody and harmony to create a unique improvisation or composition based on the given scale.

8. Repeat for other synthetic scales.

BIBLIOGRAPHY

Bach, Johann Sebastian. *371 Four-Part Chorales*. Wiesbaden, DE: Breitkopf & Härtel.

Bach, Johann Sebastian. *Keyboard Music: The Bach-Gesellschaft Edition*. New York, NY: Dover Publications, Inc., 1970.

Borroff, Edith. *Music In Europe and the United States: A History*. New York, NY: Ardsley House, 1990.

Burkholder, J. Peter, Donald Jay Grout, Claude V. Palisca. *A History of Western Music, Seventh Edition*. New York, NY: W. W. Norton & Company, 2006.

Christ, William, Richard DeLone, Vernon Kliewer, Lewis Rowell, William Thomson. *Materials and Structure of Music, Volume I*. Englewood Cliffs, NJ: Prentice-Hall, Inc., 1966.

Clendinning, Jane Piper, Elizabeth West Marvin. *Theory and Analysis, Second Edition*. New York, NY: W. W. Norton & Company, 2011.

Dobbins, Bill. *Chick Corea: Now He Sings, Now He Sobs*. Rottengurg/N. West Germany: Advance Music, 1988.

Duffin, Ross W. *How Equal Temperament Ruined Harmony (and Why You Should Care)*. New York, NY: W. W. Norton, 2007.

Edstrom, Brent. *Kenny Barron, the Collection*. Milwaukee, WI: Hal Leonard Corporation, 1996.

Edstrom, Brent. *Musicianship In the Digital Age*. Boston, MA: Thomson Course Technology PTR.

Edstrom, Brent. *Oscar Peterson Plays Standards*. Milwaukee, WI: Hal Leonard Corporation, 2008.

Haerle, Dan. *Scales for Jazz Improvisation*. Lebanon, IN: Studio P/R, Inc., 1975.

Levine, Mark. *The Jazz Theory Book*. Petaluma, CA: Sher Music Co., 1995.

Olsen, Loran. *Qillóowawya: Hitting the Rawhide*. Seattle, WA: Northwest Interpretive Association, 2001.

Persichetti, Vincent. *Twentieth-Century Harmony: Creative Aspects and Practice*. New York, NY: W. W. Norton & Company, 1961.

Ricker, Ramon. *Pentatonic Scales for Jazz Improvisation*. Lebanon, IN: Studio P/R, Inc., 1975.

Schmidt-Jones, Catherine. *Indian Classical Music: Tuning and Ragas*. OpenStax-CNX, licensed under the Creative Commons Attribution License 3.0.

Thomas, Benjamin, Michael Horvit and Robert Nelson. *Music for Analysis, Fifth Edition*. Belmont, CA: Wadsworth/Thomson Learning, 2001.

Turek, Ralph. *Analystical Anthology of Music, Second Edition*. New York, NY: McGraw-Hill, Inc., 1992.

Turek, Ralph. *The Elements of Music: Concepts and Applications, Volume One, Second Edition*. New York, NY: McGraw-Hill, Inc., 1996.

ANSWER KEY

Half Steps (page 5)

What note is a half step above B? **C**

What note is a half step below E♭? **D**

What note is a half step above F? **F♯**

What note is a half step below A? **A♭**

What note is a half step above D♭? **D**

What note is a half step below F♭? **E♭**

What note is a half step above C♭? **C**

Whole Steps (page 6)

What note is a whole step above B? **C♯**

What note is a whole step below E♭? **D♭**

What note is a whole step above F? **G**

What note is a whole step below A? **G**

What note is a whole step above D♭? **E♭**

What note is a whole step below F♭? **E♭♭ (same as D)**

What note is a whole step above C♭? **D♭**

Anatomy of a Major Scale (page 9)

Sharp   **Flat**

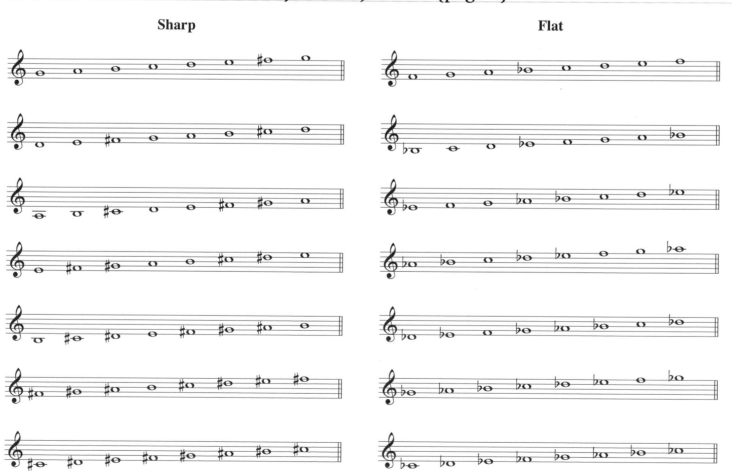

Scale-degree Identification (page 13)

What note is the supertonic of an F major scale? **G**

The note E is the supertonic in which major scale? **D**

What note is the dominant of a D major scale? **A**

The note A is the dominant in which major scale? **D**

What note is the subdominant of an E♭ major scale? **A♭**

The note B♭ is the subdominant in which major scale? **F**

What note is the mediant in of a B major scale? **D♯**

The note F♯ is the submediant in which major scale? **A**

What note is the leading tone of a G major scale? **F♯**

The note E♭ is the mediant in which major scale? **C♭**

What note is the submediant of a D♭ major scale? **B♭**

The note G♯ is the leading tone in which major scale? **A**

Minor Scales (page 15)

The relative minor of D major is **B** minor.

The relative minor of F major is **D** minor.

The relative minor of E♭ major is **C** minor.

The relative minor of B major is **G♯** minor.

The relative minor of A major is **F♯** minor.

The relative minor of D♭ major is **B♭** minor.

Scale Degrees in Minor (page 16)

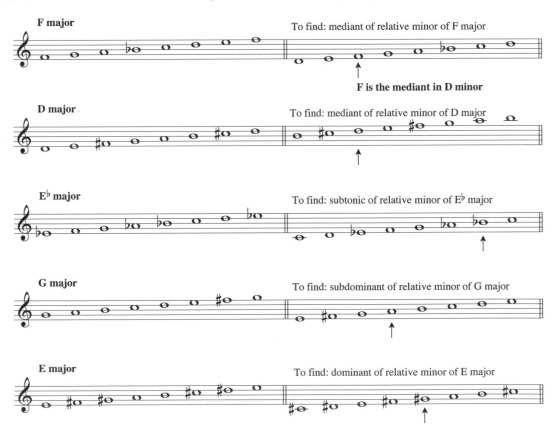

Harmonic Minor (page 17)

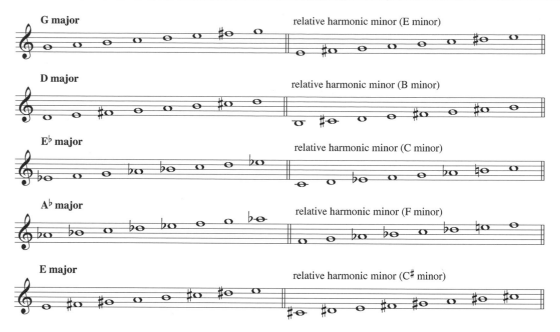

Melodic Minor (page 19)

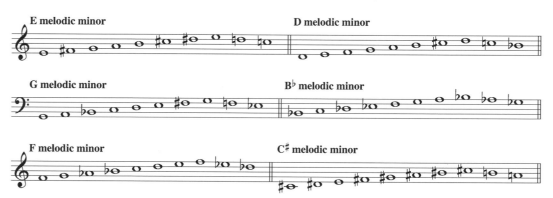

Relative Minor Scales (page 20)

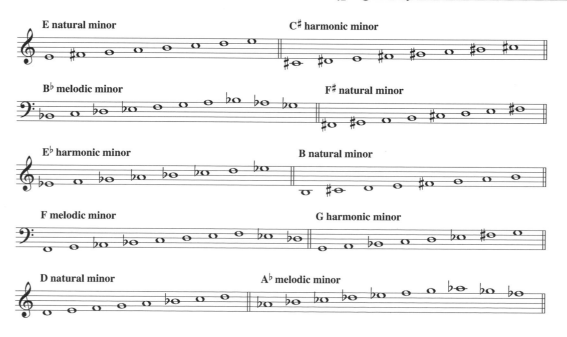

Pentatonic Scales (page 25)

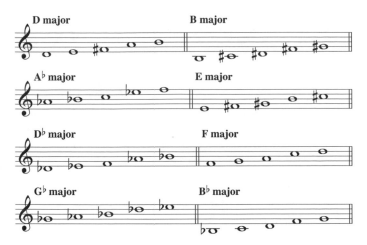

Minor Pentatonic Scales (page 27)

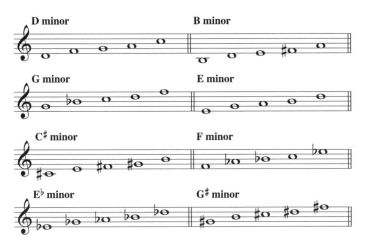

Modes (page 31)

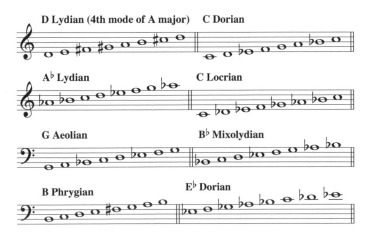

Analyzing Modal Music (page 33)

F Mixolydian

C Dorian

A Phrygian

Blues Scales (page 35)

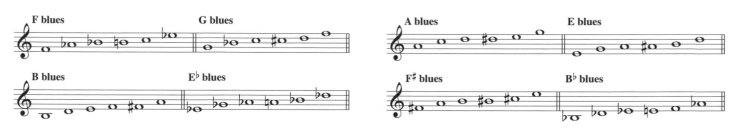

Scale-Writing Exercise (page 38)

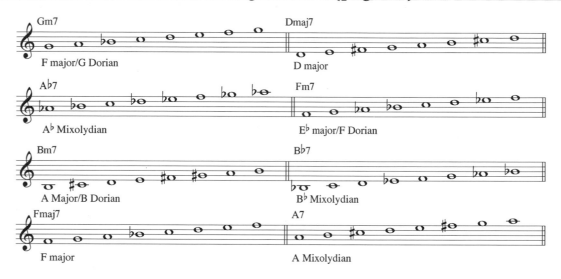

Melodic Minor Exercise (page 42)

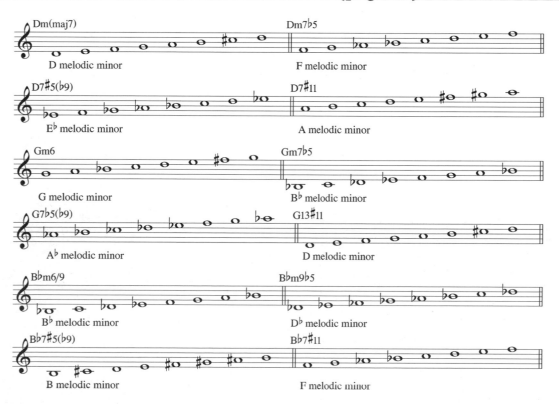

Chromatic Scale (page 44)

1.	Ascending:	A	A♯	B
2.	Descending:	G	G♭	F
3.	Ascending:	D	D♯	E
4.	Descending:	B	B♭	A
5.	Ascending:	C	C♯	D
6.	Descending:	D	D♭	C
7.	Ascending:	F	F♯	G
8.	Descending:	E	E♭	D

Synthetic Scales (page 46)

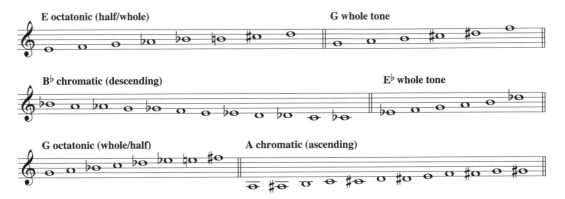

Analysis Tips (page 48)

D Octatonic (half/whole diminished)

Chromatic scale